Helping Children See Jesus

ISBN: 978-1-64104-013-6

A Little Rascal
The True Story of Anthony T. Rossi

Author: Michelle Morin   Illustrator: Debby Saint
Computer Graphic Artist: Samuel Laterza
Page Layout: Patricia Pope

© 2020 Bible Visuals International
PO Box 153, Akron, PA 17501-0153
Phone: (717) 859-1131
www.biblevisuals.org

All rights reserved. No part of this publication may be reproduced, stored in a retrieval system or transmitted in any form by any means, electronic, mechanical, photocopy, recording or otherwise, without the prior permission of the publisher, except as provided by USA copyright law.

For other formats of this story and related items, please visit www.biblevisuals.org and search using the title or the item "5272".

Chapter 1
The Day of the Terramoto

Anthony listened hard in the darkness. He heard the even breathing of his brothers, the ticking of a clock, and then—he heard *it* again, a low rumble that seemed to come from far away. The family's pet bird flapped his wings frantically against the bars of his cage. Suddenly the room began to roll and windows rattled. Tony felt as if his home were swaying back and forth as he jumped out of bed and ran down the stairs with his family.

"Terramoto!" "Earthquake!" they shouted to each other as they scrambled toward the massive doorway of their home. They clung to each other as the earthquake rumbled and the ground shook. Soon they could no longer tell the thundering noise of terramoto from the crashing of buildings and walls as they fell.

When the shaking stopped, Tony peered cautiously into the early morning dawn. Not a building was left standing in Messina, Italy. The Rossi family had nowhere to go.

"What about Aunt Emilia's house?" Mother asked as she looked at her husband. "Would we be safe there?"

The family walked to Aunt Emilia's home out in the country, but even there no one dared to stay indoors as the earthquake's aftershocks rocked the ground every five minutes. As the earth quaked, homes toppled like toy building blocks.

Hours passed. No one thought of eating. They were too afraid, and besides, there was no food as it was all buried in the ruins. But soon Tony's empty stomach grumbled. He tried the lemons on Aunt Emilia's tree, but their sour juice made his stomach cramp in pain.

The family waited for help, for food, and for news of missing relatives. Then a message came. Riccardo, Tony's older brother, had been killed in the earthquake. Tony forgot his fear and hunger. His insides felt twisted like a tight knot.

Riccardo had always been generous and caring. He had been away from home caring for a sick relative when the terramoto hit. Six-year-old Tony couldn't understand that 80,000 people had died along with his brother. All he knew was that he wanted things to be normal again. He missed his big brother so much that now his stomach ached all the time.

Finally, after three days, a rescue ship reached the island of Sicily. Now, there was bread and butter in Messina—and a way to safety. The Rossi family sailed to Syracuse, a town farther along the Sicilian coast which had not been harmed by the earthquake. There, Tony and his four brothers, his parents, and his grandmother lived in a small building until their home could be rebuilt.

Tony thought often about the earthquake. He heard his grandmother speak of Judgment Day and wondered, *Will Judgment Day be like the day of the terramoto?* Looking up into the cloudless, blue sky over Syracuse, Tony thought also about his brother. *Riccardo was good, so he is probably in heaven. If I had died, I don't think I would have gone to Heaven. I know I am not good.*

Tony was always getting into mischief. By the time the Rossi family moved back to Messina to live in barracks with other families, Tony was called "Birbanti." "Rascal." And was he a rascal!

Two years passed and one day Tony saw a "horseless carriage." He was fascinated by the car and began to run beside it. But the car gained speed and Tony's excitement grew. He wouldn't give up! The wheels of the car rolled faster and faster. Tony's legs pounded the road, his arms pumped back and forth, and he gasped for air.

What a sight it was for those who stood along the street. "Tony Rossi is racing the 'horseless carriage'," people shouted to each other. They watched in amazement as the car sped away. "Ahhh, Birbanti, that rascal boy! What will he do next?"

Tony was a rascal boy at school, too. It wasn't that he didn't like to learn. He was quick in learning to read and always solved the math problems before the other children in his class. It was just that the outdoors and adventure were on the other side of the classroom windows. Often Tony skipped school.

One morning Papa approached Tony. "Son, today I want you to go to school. Get a good start. Here is ten cents for your recess. Be a good boy. Arrivederci (goodbye)."

How could Tony skip school when Papa had been so kind? Tony resolved, *I will go to school today*.

But he had walked only one block when he saw his friend Giovanni. "Where have you been?" Tony asked, slapping his pal on the back. "I haven't seen you for days!"

"Oh," Giovanni said shrugging his shoulders, "I've been on my father's fishing boat. He wants me to go again, but I don't want to go."

Tony's gray eyes sparkled. School was forgotten. "I've got an idea," he said with excitement.

"What?"

"Let's hike over to the other side of Sicily just to see what it's like there. I've always wondered."

Giovanni grinned. "Let's go!"

The boys turned off the path that led to school. Anthony pulled his ten cents from his pocket. "How much do you have?"

"Nothing," Giovanni said.

"Well, we need more money than this," Tony said with a groan. He looked at Giovanni and then shouted, "I know! I have a cousin, a professor, who has some goldfish. We could catch and sell them!"

Off they headed to the professor's house. Tony spotted a tin can on the way and pounced on it. "We can catch the fish in this." And they did. But they could only sell half of the fish.

Pocketing the money, Tony led Giovanni to a broom closet off the barracks conference room. "We'll stay here 'til dark," Tony whispered. "Then we'll sneak into the neighbors' kitchens and steal food for our trip." The closet was cramped and dark, but Tony and Giovanni didn't mind. They were going on an adventure to the other side of Sicily!

Night fell. The boys heard Tony's brothers giving the family whistle as they searched for him. The boys huddled in the closet. When all was quiet, they tiptoed out of the barracks to the row of homes behind the building. Cautiously they slipped into a neighbor's kitchen through an unlocked door. Coffee, sugar, a candle, a cooking pot—the neighbor's house had all kinds of things they needed.

They crept out the door. A floorboard beneath them squeaked as they scampered into the night.

"Kees, Kees!" scolded a woman inside. "What is that cat doing now?" she muttered.

Panting with relief, the boys moved down the street to another house, and then another, stealing more coffee, sugar and another candle. Back in the broom closet with their loot, they waited. Tony dreamed of hiking over the Sicilian mountains where no fishing boats or school would keep him from fun and adventure.

The boys emerged from their hiding place with the early rays of sun. The grocery store was in the next block. They would buy the rest of what they needed and then be on their way.

Shouts came from behind the boys. "Tony! Tony! There he is!" Tony ran like the wind.

Tony ran as fast as he could, but he couldn't get away from the older boys. They tackled him and brought him down. Each took an arm and a leg and hauled him home. Joe grabbed his younger brother and tied him to his bed. "Now you won't get into mischief."

"You are grounded for two days, Tony," said his father sternly. "And you will spend all of those days in bed!"

Tony felt miserable. He stared at the ceiling, then glanced at the door as Grandma Rossi paused, looked in at him, and shook her head. Her "Birbanti" had a special place in her heart. Tony felt ashamed as Grandma turned away.

Two days later Grandma entered Tony's room. "You may leave your room, Birbanti."

Tony threw his arms around her neck and would have run out the door, but Grandma stopped him.

"Why, Birbanti, why do you not go to school?" she scolded. "You need an education just like all the other boys."

"I'm sorry, Grandma, for skipping school. If I could take some friends along, maybe I wouldn't mind going to school."

"But Tony, you have friends at school!" Grandma exclaimed as her grandson ran from the room.

Not the kind of friends I'd like in school, Tony thought, a plan forming in his mind.

Tony poked around the house until he found what he needed. Then he found his brother.

"Watch, Carlo, it's simple," said Tony to his brother. Tony took a short piece of bamboo and placed a hunk of cheese on one end. "This is the way to catch a mouse." He placed a pot upside down over the stick so that the pot rested on the outside end of it. Inside the pot was the cheese. The rim of the pot balanced on the edge of the stick. "See what I mean?"

Carlo looked at the contraption skeptically. "I'll believe it works if you catch a mouse in it," he said as he walked away.

Tony woke early the next morning and ran to inspect his trap. "Carlo! Carlo, we have caught a mouse!" he yelled and knelt beside the pot. He could hear scratching and scurrying noises under the pot.

Tony carefully lifted the pot. Two mice! The boys grabbed the mice and stuffed them into a paper bag. Tony's cheeks were flushed with excitement. "Come on, Carlo. Let's go to school!"

"What?" Carlo asked in surprise. "You? Go to school? And this early?" He ran after Tony and the two headed for the school.

Tony slipped into his classroom ahead of time. No one noticed when he went first to the teacher's desk or that he carried a paper bag. Then he sat quietly with the other ten-year-olds.

Class began, as usual, with recitation. The teacher stood erect and pointed her long, skinny finger straight at Tony. "Anthony Rossi, will you please repeat the poem for today?"

Tony stood. "I'm sorry. I do not know it," he said humbly and then slid into his seat as another child stood and recited the poem. As soon as the boy was finished, Tony's hand shot up. "I know it now," he blurted out.

The teacher looked at him unconvinced. "You told me, Anthony, that you could not say the poem."

"I do know it now." He stood and repeated the poem perfectly, having heard it only once.

As the teacher walked toward her desk she thought, *how encouraging this will be to tell his parents.*

She sat down behind the desk and opened her drawer. Two fuzzy mice sprang out, darted across the desk and landed in her lap.

The boys hollered with laughter while the girls shrieked. Tony sat at his desk with a smug look on his face.

But that look was gone later in the day as he walked home with a note for his father. What punishment would he get this time? *I am such a rascal*, he thought. *Papa has to punish me almost every day.*

Tony's reputation for trouble grew with every prank and mischievous deed. But something else was also growing inside Tony— an awareness that something was missing in his life.

Ever since the earthquake, the day of the terramoto, Tony had wondered about Heaven and God. Late one afternoon, Tony came in earlier than usual from play. He sat down on a low stool at Grandma Rossi's feet. His eyes studied her face. He watched as she took out her rosary. With large, questioning eyes, Tony asked, "Grandma, may I think about God with you?"

"Why, yes, Tony. We can do the rosary together."

Grandma touched a bead. "Santa Maria," she said. Tony repeated the Latin words. Usually Tony could not sit still for long, but today he sat spellbound with his Grandma Rossi's prayer beads.

Because he longed to know God, Tony never missed going to mass at church on Sunday. Somehow in the cool and quiet of his Grandma's big, dimly lit cathedral he felt as if he was doing something good instead of being a rascal. He decided to serve in the church as an altar boy.

Over the next couple of years, to the priest's surprise, the boy he knew as "rascal boy" arrived on time and always performed his duties well.

As Tony went to church, his questions went with him. One day he said aloud to no one in particular, "How can I know I am going to Heaven when I die?"

A grown-up in the church heard Tony. "Just be careful, boy, to say special prayers every morning and every evening. Don't miss a morning or evening for seven years. Then you will go to Heaven when you die."

Tony walked home with a determined look on his face. *I will say those prayers night and day*, he resolved. Sometimes, though, after a busy day of playing hard, he would flop in bed and start to pray only to fall asleep before he had finished praying. The next morning when he awoke he repeated the prayers seven times to make up for missing them the night before. *Is this enough?* he wondered. *How can I know for sure I'm doing enough?* But it seemed as if no one, not even the priest, could answer his questions.

When Tony was 14, Baby Teresa was born. Now there were eight Rossi children, but Mama didn't seem to mind. In fact, she seemed happy.

"I think Teresa looks like you, Mama," he said when the baby was two months old. As he looked at his little sister, he thought of Mama. *She really loves us. She mends my socks and clothes almost every night, long after I've gone to sleep.*

Tony was 15 when Mama became ill with cancer. On the day of Mama's death, Tony thought he would never smile again. How empty the house now felt, even with eight children and their father! Tony was miserable. He felt as if a part of him had been torn away. *Mama never had time to go to church with me. She was always busy caring for the family. If only I could have died instead of her! If only I could know God maybe I could understand about death.*

Tony became restless and looked beyond the tiny island of Sicily for new adventures. When an uncle from America visited the Rossi home, Tony spent hours with him asking one question after another.

"Was Buffalo Bill real? Is America like Sicily?"

"No," replied Uncle Constantino. "Not a bit like Sicily or Italy. Here workmen can earn only ten cents a day. Over in America almost anyone can earn a whole dollar a day."

"And New York?" Tony asked with excitement. "Can anybody find a job there, and a place to live?"

Tony now dreamed of going to America. *I will go there even if I have to swim the Atlantic*, he vowed.

And to make that dream come true, Tony got a job. He worked as a trolley conductor. It was perfect! He was always on the move now, traveling around the city of Messina.

Tony turned 17 and realized his dream of going to America would have to wait. He had to serve in the military. World War I was raging throughout Europe. The future was very uncertain.

On Tony's last day as trolley conductor, he decided to make this day unforgettable for all who rode his car. Ignoring the usual speed regulations, he raced over the downhill tracks at a screaming pitch. His terrified passengers held tightly to their seats. Tony lived up to his reputation as a rascal right up to his last day in Messina.

For the next three years Tony served in the Italian infantry without any opportunity to visit his family.

One morning, as Tony prepared to report for duty, he stepped on a rusty nail. "Ow! That hurt," he cried.

Tony tried to ignore the pain, but soon his foot throbbed. When he removed his shoe and sock, his foot was swollen and red streaks were running up his leg.

At the medical office the army doctor took one look and announced, "Blood poisoning!" He put Tony in the hospital where doctors and nurses worked to save his life. His fever raged, but finally medicine stopped the infection.

Tony began to recover gradually, but he had to stay in the hospital for a month.

"What can I do in here for a whole month?" he asked in frustration. The rascal boy might be grown up, but he still couldn't sit still.

Finally he had a thought. *Astronomy! I've always wanted to learn about the stars.* "Nurse, may I please have an astronomy book to study?"

Tony spent hours reading the book. *How wonderful God is*! he thought. *Someday perhaps I will know Him.*

When he was released from the army, he felt uneasy going home. His uncle and Grandma Rossi had died while he was in the army, Papa now had a new wife, and three of his brothers had moved away from home.

America! I will go to America! Tony decided. But every office he contacted about sailing to America told him the same line, "Our ships are booked for months. There is no room."

"I will find a way to America! I will!" Tony exclaimed.

Chapter 2
Adventures in America

Ten days after Tony contacted a shipping office he received a one-line message from the ship's captain: *one passenger is ill and can't leave tomorrow on the ship to America.*

"I will go!" Tony exclaimed. He hurried to get his passport and to borrow money for his ticket. He packed his belongings and said good bye to his family. That very day he traveled by train to Naples, Italy, where he would begin his journey across the ocean to America.

He raced up the gangplank of the huge ship, a suitcase in each hand and 30 American dollars in his pocket. His heartbeat quickened when the deep-throated whistle announced the ship's departure from the harbor.

Anthony Rossi was on his way to America! And how long the trip took from Naples, Italy, to New York City!

As the ocean liner finally approached America, Tony stood on the deck, his eyes scanning the coastline.

"There she is!" cried Tony. "The Statue of Liberty!"

Other ships and smaller crafts carved white lines of foam in the harbor's busy waters. Tony felt the excitement surge inside him as he watched businessmen, travelers from foreign lands and important-looking officers hurrying to and fro on the ship.

Twenty-one-year-old Tony could hardly wait for the ship to dock. He was ready to tackle anything, even though he could only say "please," "yes," "no" and "I am hungry" in English.

Tony found the train station with no problem. Uncle Constantino had given him directions to the home of an Italian family in New York City. "They are my friends," he had assured Tony. "They will be your friends, too."

Once on the train, Tony double checked the directions and realized he needed help.

"Please, Bleeker Street," he asked the conductor on the train.

"I'll tell you when to get off," the conductor assured him.

Traveling alone on the train, Tony couldn't talk with those around him. He didn't understand what they were saying, so he thought, *When I get off at Bleeker Street, will I find Thompson Street? Will Uncle's friends really be friendly? How long will it take me to find a job? My 30 dollars won't last long.*

The train clicked past homes and street signs and then rounded a long curve. The signs confused Tony. The view through his window did not match his uncle's directions. He stepped up to the conductor again.

"Please, Bleeker Street?"

The conductor impatiently waved his arms and gestured that they had passed Bleeker Street. "Get off at the next stop. Go back. Two stops back."

Tony got off at the next stop and looked around to see where he could catch the train going in the opposite direction. Whom should he meet but an Italian shoeshine boy! What a relief to talk Italian and get directions!

Riding in the opposite direction, Tony found Bleeker Street. With his two suitcases in his hands and his head high, Tony walked confidently away from the train station. Ahead of him was a signpost and it read "Thompson Street."

What a welcome Tony received! The warm hubbub of Italian voices assured Tony he was among friends.

"Yes, we know of your father," one of Uncle's friends cried.

Another added, "There is a job for you at our uncle's machine shop not far away. We will send someone along with you to make arrangements."

Tony met the mechanic that afternoon. "You will hand me tools when I need them, help me with construction projects and learn my trade," the mechanic told him. "Be here at seven o'clock tomorrow morning, young man. Arrivederci!"

Now Tony needed a place to stay. But his new friends had arranged for that, too. "Tony, there is an Italian family on West Broadway. They have an apartment on the sixth floor. They say there is room for you to board there."

After only a few hours in America, Tony had a job, a place to stay and friends!

New York winters were bitterly cold. Tony shivered under his sheets as the alarm clock clanged. He watched the key unwind on the clock, then jumped out of bed. His bare feet hit the icy floorboards. "Brrrr," he exclaimed, dressing quickly. "Sure wish I could have a pot of hot chicken soup all cooked and ready when I come home tonight."

Tony hurried to the kitchen to prepare his breakfast. As he turned on the gas stove, an idea entered his mind. Excitedly he went to his bedroom, grabbed his alarm clock and returned to the stove. Getting some string he tied the legs of the alarm to the left burner on the stove. Then he tied a cord to the wind up key on the clock. Taking the other end of the cord, he fastened it to the stove handle.

Tony lit the gas, turned on the stove, and then set off the alarm to test his invention. Sure enough, the clock spun the cord around its wind up key so the stove handle slowly, but surely, was pulled into the off position.

"A fresh chicken, water, salt, an onion, some vegetables," Tony listed the ingredients as he placed them in a pan. "Now, the soup will have to cook for about three hours," he decided as he set the alarm. "When I come home tonight, I'll only have to heat the soup." Tony laughed as he left his apartment and ran down the six flights of steps.

Tony's next challenge was driving a taxi cab. After only six months in the United States, he bought his own car. Soon he left his job in the machine shop.

Driving through New York City one day Tony thought, *Taxi driving is great, but with another kind of car, I could become a chauffeur. That might be even better!* Tony took his savings and bought a bigger car, then began looking for someone who needed a chauffeur.

Knock. Knock. Knock.

Tony rapped firmly on Mr. Root's door. Wealthy and the owner of a grand home, Mr. Root had a reputation for being stuffy and proud. He would not read a newspaper without wearing gloves. He spoke to others only when he could not avoid it.

But Mr. Root needed a chauffeur, and Tony applied in person. He would not be bullied by Mr. Root's haughtiness.

Mr. Root looked down his nose at Tony. "How much do you charge per month for your car and your services?"

Without blinking an eye, Tony stated, "$450 a month, sir." Only a year ago, Tony had been earning just $140 a month at the machine shop.

"Well, hum, that's rather much, don't you think?" Mr. Root's eyebrows shot up.

Tony didn't respond.

"I tell you, young man, $450 is a lot of money! Think it over and telephone me if you change your mind."

"Yes," Tony answered seriously.

Mr. Root sensed Tony would not call with a lower price. "I will phone you if I decide it is a deal," he stated.

When Tony reached his apartment, the phone was ringing. Mr. Root had made his decision. "Meet me at my home at 1:15 sharp," he barked into the phone.

Tony began his new job enthusiastically. Mr. Root never spoke to him as they drove. He rang a bell once for Tony to stop the car; two rings meant turn right; three rings meant turn left. With no one to talk to, Tony had time to think and lots of ideas were brewing in Birbanti's mind.

Why not take a part-time job too? Tony asked himself. So he collected eggs

in the country and sold them door-to-door in the city. When Tony's brother, Joe, arrived from Italy, they opened a grocery store and advertised their specialty: Aurora Farms–Eggs only one day old.

Aurora Farms became popular. Tony had a knack for remembering prices, getting along with his customers and finding the best deals. Even though it was Depression times (late 1920s) and many stores had closed, Aurora Farms grew. One day a man came to the store and offered Tony $30,000 for the store and all the groceries.

Tony thought, *I've enjoyed Aurora Farms, but I've always wanted to try the restaurant business.* So he sold the store.

About a year after opening his first restaurant, Tony noticed that his old store had closed.

"What happened?" he asked a person he met on the street near the store.

"Just gave up, they did. Store didn't do well, so they left," the man replied before walking on.

Tony remembered his happy days at Aurora Farms and made another split-second decision. He turned to his brother, "Joe, I'm leaving the restaurant in your hands and I'm going back to Aurora Farms."

Once again the store became popular. Tony's old customers were thrilled to have him back in the neighborhood. And Tony enjoyed meeting new customers, too. There was a young lady who shopped regularly at the store. To Tony, whenever she entered the store, it was as if all the other customers disappeared.

I've never met anyone like her before, Tony marveled. His rascally mind began working. *I wonder how I can get to know her.*

Tony stood beside the cash register staring into space. Suddenly he looked up to see Florence Stark standing at the counter with her groceries. Her eyes were smiling. "May I leave these groceries here?" she asked. "I need to go to the butcher shop, so I'll pick them up when I come back."

"Why, certainly," Tony stammered.

While Florence bought her meat, Birbanti hurried around the store. He hunted until he found several large jars of jelly. Then, he put them in the bottom of the bag containing Florence's groceries. He smiled to himself. *She won't be able to lift this bag now*, he reasoned.

When Florence returned, she was startled to find the bag so heavy. "I didn't think I bought so much," she said with surprise.

"Never mind, Miss Stark," Tony replied, hoping he looked cool and casual. "I will have them sent to your apartment."

"Why, thank you!" Florence exclaimed. "I appreciate your service very, very much."

Later, who should deliver the bag of groceries to Florence's apartment but Tony himself.

Soon Tony and Florence realized how much they liked each other. Tony proposed and Florence accepted. When the months of their long engagement were over, Tony was ecstatic! He had married the woman he loved, he was still in his 30s, and he had one of the most successful grocery stores in New York City.

One day, however, Tony asked Florence, "Have you ever been to Florida?"

By now, Florence had learned that a tiny bit of young Birbanti the Rascal Boy lived on in her hard-working husband. Tony never stopped dreaming.

"If we go South," he continued, "I think I would like to try farming."

"What kind of farming?" she asked, mystified.

"I don't know exactly. I think I will go to the library and find out about agriculture in the South, especially in Florida."

Tony was so committed to his new adventure that he sold the store. With his free time he prepared to move south. He loved to visit the New York City Public Library and was fascinated by what he discovered there about growing tomatoes.

He took a book to a long wooden table and sat to read. Someone before him had left a book on the table. Tony glanced at it and the title captured his interest.

The Life of Christ, Tony said to himself. *I don't know anything about Christ except what I learned as a child at Christmas and Easter times.* He opened the book and began to read. He couldn't put the book down! On and on he read, forgetting all about his book on tomato farming. The story of Jesus' life unfolded as Tony read. Hours passed. Tony looked at his watch. He'd read through lunchtime. Quickly he ran out to get a sandwich. Then, he hurried back to the library to read more.

As the late afternoon sun began streaming in the windows and library workers began tidying up for closing time, Tony realized that he had read for the entire day! *This is wonderful!* he thought as he closed the book and stretched. *But, now, why don't I go to the source? Tomorrow I'll come back and find a Bible to read.*

Tony returned the next day, and the next. He read of God's power in creating the world. *How great a God to create this vast universe,* thought Tony as he remembered the astronomy book he had read years ago.

He continued reading about God's faithfulness and fairness with His people in the Old Testament, but was so excited to move on to the New Testament that he began skipping sections.

"Finally," he sighed. "The first book of the New Testament on the life of Christ." Tony was not disappointed. The miracles of Jesus, His wise teaching, His death on the cross and the way He came to life again impressed Tony greatly. Then he read the words of John 3:16. *For God so loved the world, that He gave His only begotten Son, that whosoever believeth in him should not perish, but have everlasting life.*

Suddenly all the questions Tony had had about God over the years were answered. *Here it is!* he cried to himself. *Christ has already died to pay for all my sins. He will forgive each person who trusts Him.*

The library was very quiet as Tony pondered what he had read. He knew God was real. And now he understood that all he needed to do was believe that Jesus had died for his sin.

He bowed his head. In the silence surrounding him God seemed very near. *God, you know that I have always been the Rascal Boy. Even now I put my work and myself first. Thank You for giving Your Son to be punished for my sin. I want you to be my Saviour. I want to put You first now, ahead of my work, ahead of dear Florence and ahead of myself.*

Tony left the library with a smile on his face. He hurried home to tell Florence what he had done. *I wonder how following Jesus will change my big plans for success*, Tony thought.

Chapter 3
Anthony Rossi, Entrepreneur and Christian

"You can't pay your men a dollar a day!" complained the farmer. "It's hard on the rest of us. We pay 75 cents."

Tony had started tomato farming in Florida. The other farmers in the area were not pleased with his methods. But Tony was sure he was doing the right thing. He talked to God about everything he did now.

Looking over his tomato fields, he prayed, "Father, if I earn $5,000 from growing my tomatoes, I'll be satisfied."

When the tomatoes began growing, it looked like Tony would earn far more than $5,000. But when it was time to harvest the tomatoes, Tony was frustrated.

"Florence, it's impossible to find the pickers we need!" he told his wife one night. "The other farmers have already hired all the workers. And we're running out of boxes to hold the tomatoes."

Tony worked hard, but many tomatoes lay rotting on the ground. When Florence totaled their sales, she exclaimed, "Tony, we have made exactly $5,000!"

"God did just what I asked, Florence!" Tony was grateful to God. But his "Birbanti" ways were not gone. "I should have asked God for $10,000!" he said with a smile.

After seeing that God does answer prayer, Tony brought a bigger question to God. "Farming or business? Which should I do? I like both!"

One morning he walked down a street in Bradenton, Florida, when a friend called out to him and crossed the street. "Say, Tony, did you know that restaurant over there is for sale?"

Tony's heart beat fast. Could this be God's answer already? This was exciting! God was leading him.

Tony talked with his lawyer; then he and Florence opened the restaurant in Bradenton. And it was a success! God led Tony in every decision.

With the restaurant going well, Tony's mind turned to new ideas. He remembered how popular Florida oranges were with his customers at Aurora Farms in New York. *I know what I'll do,* Tony thought. *I'll sell Florida oranges to restaurants in the north.*

Tony studied the process of shipping oranges and discovered he could improve on the method and sell more than anyone else. He made sure he got the best fruit by shopping himself, and he sold his oranges for less than his competitors.

Tony's oranges were in great demand, but Tony wasn't satisfied. "I will sell fresh fruit salad and orange juice to hotels in New York City," he announced, and immediately planned how to make this idea work.

Gathering his workers around him, Tony explained, "Refrigerated trucks are not cold enough. The fruit will spoil if we use them. We'll pack the fruit and juice into a trailer truck. Then we'll blow chipped ice into it so that it is packed solidly. After that we'll cover everything with a thick canvas. I'm sure the shipment will arrive fresh in New York, even after the long trip from Florida." Workers shook their heads in amazement.

Tony was right! Soon he had dozens of trucks traveling up and down the east coast carrying fruit and juice. His new business, Tropicana ®, was growing as fast as the juice could be shipped to waiting customers.

In the midst of all this success, Florence became ill. Although she was only in her forties, Florence had a serious heart problem. As her condition worsened, she suffered a major heart attack and was rushed to the hospital. There was nothing the staff could do. Florence died as Tony held her hand.

Tony's heart ached with loneliness. He spent more and more time at Tropicana where he solved problems, built equipment and worked long into the nights.

Studying the Bible alone and with his friends kept Tony close to God. He invited friends to his home and together they read the Bible. They discussed what they read. Sometimes friends wanted to read books other than the Bible, but Tony said, "No." He reminded everyone how he had discovered Christ through reading the Bible in the New York City Library.

One day as he was praying for some of his friends who were missionaries, Tony had a thought. *I can use the money I earn from Tropicana to help missionaries!* As the thought grew, so did his excitement.

Then one day he knew that it was not enough just to help others share the good news about Jesus. *I must share this message with all my brothers and sisters in Sicily,* he told himself. *I believe they will listen. But I don't know how to tell my father about Jesus. Who am I to teach him? How can I explain it all to him?*

As Tony flew toward Sicily, he gazed out the airplane window at the dark Atlantic Ocean below. It had been 30 years since he had seen his family. Now he was a 57-year-old businessman. How would his family receive him? *Lord,* he prayed, *give me wisdom. Show me what to say and how to begin.*

Tony's attempts to share his faith with his brothers and sisters did not go well. Each time he tried to speak with them, they thought of an urgent errand and off they went. But what of Papa? Was he listening to anything Tony said?

As the whole family gathered for a meal, Tony prayed and thanked God for bringing the family together. He closed by saying, "I pray in the name of Jesus Christ, my Saviour."

When everyone lifted his head, Tony looked at Papa. The old gentleman's eyes were wet with tears. "Son," he said, "from now on I will pray in the name of Jesus Christ, my Savior."

God has heard my prayer! Papa does believe! Tony rejoiced.

When he returned to Florida, Tony worked with greater enthusiasm. Soon Tropicana had grown to 800 employees.

"Let's celebrate!" Tony declared. A party was planned to applaud their success and celebrate the new cold storage building that had just been completed.

The hum of voices and the festive sound of music filled the great room as proud employees congratulated one another on their accomplishments. Under the lights and decorations, no one could've guessed that their roof, freshly tarred that day, was smoldering red hot. Plumes of smoke danced, spreading from one end of the roof to the other. As the last people left the party and headed for their cars, the roof of the new building burst into flames. Black smoke rolled toward the sky, then the scream of sirens drowned the shocked cries of Tropicana's employees.

"Save the storage building! Wet down the roof!" cried people to each other and the firefighters.

The firefighters worked quickly, but could not save the new building. "I'm sorry, Mr. Rossi," one said.

But Tony smiled through his tears as he said, "God has decided to make Tropicana a great company. It is my job to keep working hard, thinking and praying all the time. We will rebuild."

As Tony walked to his car, he was exhausted, but another idea was forming in his mind. *I've been looking at all our refrigerated trucks tonight. Even with the whole fleet, we're not going to be able to meet the demand for Tropicana orange juice. I think I'll buy a ship. It will carry two million gallons of juice.*

Three years later Tony's ship, the *SS Tropicana*, was ready to carry the first fresh-squeezed orange juice by sea.

"I believe God gave me this idea," Tony shared with those around him. Then he grinned. "Besides, I never studied engineering. So how could I know this could NOT be done?"

With a ship to carry juice, Tropicana grew even faster. But so did Tony's desire to serve the Lord. And another idea grew, too. Some people had heard him say, "If I ever marry again, my wife must be a missionary!"

Eight years after Florence had died, Tony met Sanna Barlow, a missionary to South Africa. It wasn't long before he knew God wanted them to marry. Sanna left her missionary work in Africa and met Tony in London where they were married. Then they headed to Italy to visit Tony's family. Tony told Sanna, "I want to introduce you to my family, and I want to introduce my own people to Jesus Christ."

In Italy Tony and Sanna started a small Bible study, then a Bible conference for two hundred people. Every year they traveled back to Sicily for their vacation and each year the crowds grew at the conference. A Bible church was begun in Messina, Tony's boyhood town.

Back in Florida, the orange crop was destroyed by freezing temperatures. Tony listened to his workers. "We'll have to make our juice like everyone else. We'll be forced to buy it already squeezed in Brazil!"

"Never!" countered Tony. "Our product is 100% pure fresh-chilled juice. We cannot change. We will buy our oranges from Mexico."

Tony designed the *Mexican Pride*, a floating juice factory built from an old barge. It floated off the coast of Mexico, processing oranges into juice which was then shipped to the United States.

In the Bradenton plant one day, Tony watched the labeling machines decorate bottles. "These won't do," he said to an employee.

"But they are the best on the market, sir."

"That might be, but they don't work fast enough to decorate our bottles. Send the machine back!"

"But sir," the employee gasped, "what will we do?"

"We'll think about it," Tony replied. "God will give an answer."

A few days later Tony awoke at four o'clock in the morning. He knelt by his bed and prayed, "Dear Lord, You could help me to understand how we can have a decorator machine that is right for us."

At breakfast, the Rossis were quiet. Tony was deep in thought. They read the Bible together. Then, instead of hurrying out the door to Tropicana, Tony sat, eyes closed, lips moving.

"I've got it! I've got it!"

"What have you gotten?" Sanna asked.

"Just exactly what we want!" He dashed to the car, waving a goodbye kiss.

Immediately upon reaching his office, Tony called for his chief engineer. "This is a sketch of my idea," he said to the puzzled employee. "I think it will decorate bottles ten times faster than the other machines."

"Mr. Rossi," the engineer warned, "it isn't possible."

"Impossible? Of course, it's possible. Look, here's the way it will go."

In spite of his doubts, the engineer took the plans and studied them. *Maybe the boss has come up with another first,* he told himself.

He was right! The new machine worked perfectly.

Once again the guidelines of the Bible helped Tony to be a successful businessman. *After all,* he thought, *the Bible does say "If any man lack wisdom, let him ask of God"* (James 1:5).

Tropicana grew and grew. Tony received national awards and honors. His face was on the cover of important business magazines. Anthony Rossi was a BIG success. But in his heart, Tony knew everything he had came from God.

When he was in his seventies, Tony often said, "Lord, You know my heart is for You." And the Lord seemed to respond by giving him more ideas.

When a larger company offered to buy Tropicana, Tony thought, *If I ask a really high price, it will discourage them if they are not really serious.* But five hundred million dollars was not too high and Tropicana was sold.

Again Tony prayed, "Lord, show me how I can serve You now."

Long before selling Tropicana, Tony had a dream of building a village where retired missionaries could live free of charge for the rest of their lives. Tony was involved and excited throughout each phase of the planning and construction.

Then one day, Bradenton Missionary Village was completed–more than 100 houses with 235 apartments.

Along with the retired missionaries who moved into the village, something else moved in January 1981.

Tony's great love for the Bible led him to start an organization to bring the Word of God to those who could not read it for themselves–the blind. He called the new organization Bible Alliance (now Aurora Ministries) and moved it to the village campus.

"We will record the Bible on tape for those who cannot see well enough to read," he told his friends.

The tapes were provided free of charge. Before long people in foreign lands were requesting tapes in their language. It was difficult for Tony and the staff to convince people that the tapes were free.

One day Tony announced to the staff, "I believe there's also a use for our tapes in US prisons. Let's try it!"

Tony's many inventions made him a great success and a member of two Halls of Fame (Florida Citrus and Florida Agriculture), but he never forgot that his greatest success came from serving God.

[In this illustration, Anthony Rossi stands between blind people on the left and prisoners on the right. He holds the tapes produced by Bible Alliance.]

Epilogue

Anthony Rossi died January 1993 at the age of 92.

Just as Anthony Rossi received business awards for all his hard work, you may have received awards for your success in sports or good grades at school. Anthony used his success to show others how great God is. He felt that as great as his company (Tropicana) was, his greatest accomplishment was the work which he did for the Lord.

If God gives you success and awards, will you decide to use them to show others how great God is as Anthony Rossi did? Maybe you are the champion in a spelling contest or your picture took first place in an art contest. When people compliment you for your achievement, you could say, "Thank you, but I want the honor to go to God because He helped me. I did my best for Him."

Stay close to God by studying the Bible and praying. Try to do your very best for God as if you are working or studying for Him and not people. When success comes, use it to show others how great God is.

But seek ye first the kingdom of God, and His righteousness; and all these things shall be added unto you.

Matthew 6:33

Review Questions for *A Little Rascal*

Chapter 1

1. What country does Tony come from? *(Italy)*
2. What woke the family up early in the morning? *(An earthquake–a terramoto)*
3. Who did Tony lose in the earthquake? *(His older brother Ricardo)*
4. Why was Tony given the nickname "Birbanti"? What does it mean? *(He was always getting into mischief. It means "Rascal.")*
5. Name one of Tony's pranks. *(Chasing the "horseless carriage"; plotting his adventure to the other side of Sicily; catching the mice and putting them in the teacher's desk)*
6. What could Tony recite from memory after hearing it only once? *(A poem)*
7. Tony was thinking about God and Heaven as he grew up. What was the question that he really wanted to know the answer to? *("How can I know that I am going to Heaven when I die?")*
8. When Tony was 15, he lost someone very important. Who was it? *(His mother)*
9. Tony had a big dream to go somewhere. Where was it? *(America–even if he had to swim the Atlantic Ocean)*
10. While Tony was recovering from the blood poisoning in the hospital, what book did he read that made such an impression on him and what thoughts of God did he have while reading it? *(A book on stars–astronomy; "How wonderful God is." "Someday perhaps I will know Him.")*

Chapter 2

1. What did Tony see as the ship pulled into New York harbor? *(The Statue of Liberty)*
2. What happened to Tony on the train? *(The conductor forgot to tell Tony when to get off; an Italian shoeshine boy gave him directions when he did get off the train.)*
3. What three things did Tony have right after meeting his uncle's friends in New York City? *(A job, a place to stay, friends)*
4. What did Tony invent with an alarm clock, a cord, and the gas stove? *(A way to cook his chicken soup while he was at work)*
5. Can you name the first three jobs Tony had in the city? *(Helper in machine shop; taxi driver; a chauffeur)*
6. What did Tony do with all the eggs that he collected in the country? *(He sold them door-to-door and then started a successful grocery store along with his brother.)*
7. Why did Tony the rascal put heavy jars of jelly in Florence's grocery bags? *(They would be too heavy for her to carry home. Then Tony could do it and get to see her again.)*
8. Where did Tony want to go after they were married and what did he want to do? *(Florida; to raise tomatoes)*
9. What was the special place Tony liked to go to read up on his interests? *(The New York Public Library)*
10. After reading the Bible at the Library, whom did he meet? What Bible verse was special? *(Jesus; God's Son and Tony's Saviour; John 3:16)*

Chapter 3

1. What was Tony's first farming / business adventure in Florida? *(He grew tomatoes.)*
2. How did Tony involve God in all his business adventures? *(He talked to God about everything; he asked God for wisdom.)*
3. One of Tony's next business adventures was selling orange juice and fruit in New York and other regions. What was the name of his company? *(Tropicana ®)* How did he get the fruit there without spoiling? *(Trailer trucks with ice packed all around the fruit)*
4. What happened to his wife, Florence? *(She died from a heart attack.)*
5. Why did Tony Rossi fly home to see his family in Sicily, Italy? *(He wanted to make sure they all knew about Jesus' saving work on the cross)* What did his father say? *("Son, from now on I will pray in the name of Jesus Christ, my Saviour.")*
6. What did he buy to carry two million gallons of juice in? *(He bought a ship–the S.S. Tropicana.)*
7. Who did God send to be a help to Tony? *(Sanna, a missionary to South Africa)*
8. What did God give Tony wisdom about the problem with labeling the bottles of juice? *(He came up with a way to label /decorate the bottles 10 times faster.)*
9. Can you name two more things God led Tony to do after he sold Tropicana®? *(He built a large place where retired missionaries could live; he made tapes of the Bible for blind people and prisoners in jail.)*
10. Fill in the blank: "Tony never forgot that his greatest success came from serving _____." *(God)*

www.ingramcontent.com/pod-product-compliance
Lightning Source LLC
Chambersburg PA
CBHW042017080426
42735CB00002B/87